The humours of New Tunbridge Wells at Islington. A lyric poem. With songs, epigrams, &c, also imitations from French, Gascoon, Italian, Latin, and Chinese poets: and an ode, from a manuscript of Mr. de Voltaire.

John Lockman

ECCO
PRINT EDITIONS

The humours of New Tunbridge Wells at Islington. A lyric poem. With songs, epigrams, &c, also imitations from French, Gascoon, Italian, Latin, and Chinese poets: and an ode, from a manuscript of Mr. de Voltaire.

Lockman, John
ESTCID: T061930
Reproduction from British Library
The author in the preface gives his names as James Drake, i.e. John Lockman; the pseudonym was probably intended to mock Stephen
Duck. A shorter version appears under the title 'The charms of dishabille, or New Tunbridge Wells at Islington' in George Bic
London : printed for J. Roberts, 1734.
[16],96p.,plate ; 8°

Eighteenth Century
Collections Online
Print Editions

Gale ECCO Print Editions

Relive history with *Eighteenth Century Collections Online*, now available in print for the independent historian and collector. This series includes the most significant English-language and foreign-language works printed in Great Britain during the eighteenth century, and is organized in seven different subject areas including literature and language; medicine, science, and technology; and religion and philosophy. The collection also includes thousands of important works from the Americas.

The eighteenth century has been called "The Age of Enlightenment." It was a period of rapid advance in print culture and publishing, in world exploration, and in the rapid growth of science and technology – all of which had a profound impact on the political and cultural landscape. At the end of the century the American Revolution, French Revolution and Industrial Revolution, perhaps three of the most significant events in modern history, set in motion developments that eventually dominated world political, economic, and social life.

In a groundbreaking effort, Gale initiated a revolution of its own: digitization of epic proportions to preserve these invaluable works in the largest online archive of its kind. Contributions from major world libraries constitute over 175,000 original printed works. Scanned images of the actual pages, rather than transcriptions, recreate the works *as they first appeared.*

Now for the first time, these high-quality digital scans of original works are available via print-on-demand, making them readily accessible to libraries, students, independent scholars, and readers of all ages.

For our initial release we have created seven robust collections to form one the world's most comprehensive catalogs of 18th century works.

Initial Gale ECCO Print Editions collections include:

History and Geography
Rich in titles on English life and social history, this collection spans the world as it was known to eighteenth-century historians and explorers. Titles include a wealth of travel accounts and diaries, histories of nations from throughout the world, and maps and charts of a world that was still being discovered. Students of the War of American Independence will find fascinating accounts from the British side of conflict.

Social Science

Delve into what it was like to live during the eighteenth century by reading the first-hand accounts of everyday people, including city dwellers and farmers, businessmen and bankers, artisans and merchants, artists and their patrons, politicians and their constituents. Original texts make the American, French, and Industrial revolutions vividly contemporary.

Medicine, Science and Technology

Medical theory and practice of the 1700s developed rapidly, as is evidenced by the extensive collection, which includes descriptions of diseases, their conditions, and treatments. Books on science and technology, agriculture, military technology, natural philosophy, even cookbooks, are all contained here.

Literature and Language

Western literary study flows out of eighteenth-century works by Alexander Pope, Daniel Defoe, Henry Fielding, Frances Burney, Denis Diderot, Johann Gottfried Herder, Johann Wolfgang von Goethe, and others. Experience the birth of the modern novel, or compare the development of language using dictionaries and grammar discourses.

Religion and Philosophy

The Age of Enlightenment profoundly enriched religious and philosophical understanding and continues to influence present-day thinking. Works collected here include masterpieces by David Hume, Immanuel Kant, and Jean-Jacques Rousseau, as well as religious sermons and moral debates on the issues of the day, such as the slave trade. The Age of Reason saw conflict between Protestantism and Catholicism transformed into one between faith and logic -- a debate that continues in the twenty-first century.

Law and Reference

This collection reveals the history of English common law and Empire law in a vastly changing world of British expansion. Dominating the legal field is the *Commentaries of the Law of England* by Sir William Blackstone, which first appeared in 1765. Reference works such as almanacs and catalogues continue to educate us by revealing the day-to-day workings of society.

Fine Arts

The eighteenth-century fascination with Greek and Roman antiquity followed the systematic excavation of the ruins at Pompeii and Herculaneum in southern Italy; and after 1750 a neoclassical style dominated all artistic fields. The titles here trace developments in mostly English-language works on painting, sculpture, architecture, music, theater, and other disciplines. Instructional works on musical instruments, catalogs of art objects, comic operas, and more are also included.

The BiblioLife Network

This project was made possible in part by the BiblioLife Network (BLN), a project aimed at addressing some of the huge challenges facing book preservationists around the world. The BLN includes libraries, library networks, archives, subject matter experts, online communities and library service providers. We believe every book ever published should be available as a high-quality print reproduction; printed on-demand anywhere in the world. This insures the ongoing accessibility of the content and helps generate sustainable revenue for the libraries and organizations that work to preserve these important materials.

The following book is in the "public domain" and represents an authentic reproduction of the text as printed by the original publisher. While we have attempted to accurately maintain the integrity of the original work, there are sometimes problems with the original work or the micro-film from which the books were digitized. This can result in minor errors in reproduction. Possible imperfections include missing and blurred pages, poor pictures, markings and other reproduction issues beyond our control. Because this work is culturally important, we have made it available as part of our commitment to protecting, preserving, and promoting the world's literature.

GUIDE TO FOLD-OUTS MAPS and OVERSIZED IMAGES

The book you are reading was digitized from microfilm captured over the past thirty to forty years. Years after the creation of the original microfilm, the book was converted to digital files and made available in an online database.

In an online database, page images do not need to conform to the size restrictions found in a printed book. When converting these images back into a printed bound book, the page sizes are standardized in ways that maintain the detail of the original. For large images, such as fold-out maps, the original page image is split into two or more pages

Guidelines used to determine how to split the page image follows:

• Some images are split vertically; large images require vertical and horizontal splits.
• For horizontal splits, the content is split left to right.
• For vertical splits, the content is split from top to bottom.
• For both vertical and horizontal splits, the image is processed from top left to bottom right.

Caprice

New Tunbridge Wells near Islington

K Dzuka parrus/

THE
HUMOURS

OF

New Tunbridge Wells

AT

ISLINGTON.

A

Lyric P O E M.

WITH

SONGS, EPIGRAMS, &c,

ALSO

Imitations from *French, Gafcoon, Italian, Latin,*
and *Chinefe* Poets:

AND

An Ode, from a Manufcript of Mr. *de* VOLTAIRE.

Video meliora, proboque;
Deteriora fequor.   Ovid. Met.

L O N D O N:
Printed for J. ROBERTS, at the *Oxford* Arms in *War-
wick Lane.* MDCCXXXIV.
Price 1 *s.* 6 *d.*

T O

Mr. de VOLTAIRE.

S I R,

YOU, no doubt, will be very much
surprized at this publick Addreſs,
from One who has not the Happineſs
of being perſonally known to you; but a
Genius like yours can no more eſcape In-
truſions of this Nature, than a fine Woman
can ſecure her ſelf from importunate Enco-
miums. Beauty makes the ſtrongeſt Im-
preſſion on all but the Blind and the Taſte-
leſs; and Thoſe who are affected by its
Power, can ſcarce refrain teſtifying, by
ſome outward Demonſtration, the exquiſite
Delight they enjoy from its Influence. I
am one of the innumerable Readers who
have received uncommon Pleaſure from
your Muſe, which is one Reaſon why I
wou'd gratefully attempt to draw the Idea

I have

DEDICATION.

I have form'd of her Charms; but on this Occasion I find the Expression so vastly faint in Comparison of what I feel, that my Endeavour to describe her Graces wou'd be doing them the highest Injury, and therefore 'twill much better become me to admire them in Silence.

But I'm afraid 'twill not be thought I have in any manner improv'd the Compliment, when I desire your Acceptance of the following Sheets, For,

Fond of the Parnassian *Shade,*
In Fancy's wild Parterre I stray'd;
Thence Flowers I cull'd of various Dyes,
And pleas'd with my ideal Prize,
For once, impertinently-free,
Prepar'd the gayest Wreathe for Thee.

And indeed, I am but too conscious that such Pieces in the ensuing Collection as are more immediately my own, are far from being worthy of your Patronage; but nevertheless I hope from your Candor, that the Intention with which I offer them,

may

may attone in some measure for their Imperfections.

No one was ever more passionately smit with the Love of the Muses than I have been, nor ever was Creature more unluckily cross'd in it, for alas!

With Sickness and a Train of Ills opprest,
In vain the warbling Nine inform'd my
   Breast;
Deny'd each Joy that fans the Poet's Flame,
Yet eagerly I sought the Charmer, Fame;
From my Pursuit the coy bright Vision flew,
And with her, every lovely Hope withdrew.
Then darkling, sad, unpatroniz'd I rove,
Forbid the Mazes of the vocal Grove;
Like Psyche, *by the God of Love beguil'd,*
(The Glories vanish'd) languish in the Wild.

And in the Wild I for ever might have languish'd, had not you been so indulgent as to take some notice of me; a Circumstance I, unhappily, cannot declare to the World, without at the same time paying the highest Compliment to my self.

But

DEDICATION.

But to prevent the Publick from making any improper Conjectures on this Occasion, it may be necessary to inform them of the signal Obligations I have to your Muse. You was pleased to let me teach her the *English* Tongue. To her delightfully-instructive Conversation I chiefly owe whatever Improvement I may have made in Taste and the *Belles Lettres*: Her amiable Encouragement rais'd my drooping Genius to Heights it, till then, had never attain'd; and the Reputation of so illustrious an Acquaintance, procur'd me Access to such Poets as are the Ornament of the Age.

The Wren thus meditates a lonely Flight;
Silent she rises, scarcely lost to Sight,
Till by the Eagle wafted far on high,
Singing she basks in the sublimest Sky;
Hails Phœbus; wantons round his glit-
    tering Lyre,
Amid the noblest of the feather'd Choir.

After this Confession, how vain soever it may be thought, no Person, I presume, can
object

DEDICATION.

object to the Propriety of this Dedication. I cou'd only wish that, in return for your great Favours, some Opportunity would present it self, by which I might prove how sincerely I am,

SIR,

Your most obedient Servant,

THE

THE

PREFACE.

THE facetious Author of A Tale of a Tub observes, " That some things " are extremely witty to day, or " fasting, or in this Place, or at eight a " Clock, or over a Bottle, or spoke by " Mr. What d'y call'm, or in a Summer's " Morning: any of which, by the smallest " Transposal or Misapplication, is utterly " annihilate."—— I don't doubt but these humorous Reflections may very justly be applied to the following (I had like to have said Ode) Ballad, Poem; or by what Title soever the Reader may please to dignify or distinguish it, on New Tunbridge Wells. Very possibly, what was thought pretty enough, as the Phrase is, over a Glass of Water at the Spring, or over a Dish of Coffee in the Breakfast Rooms, when those Wells were in their Glory, will now appear as cold, as languid and insipid as the pre-

PREFACE.

sent Season. To confess the Truth, I myself, at this present writing, don't find the hundredth Part of the Vivacity, Humour and Spirit in my Descriptions, as I did when I drew them on the Spot, (for on the Spot they were drawn, and without the usual Assistance of Pen, Ink, Paper, Pencil, or even Chalk; a Circumstance I earnestly intreat the candid and erudite Reader to mark attentively, for divers and sundry weighty Reasons, which I'll disclose to Him the very first time we get over a Bottle;) and therefore, I say, shan't be much astonish'd, shou'd those Descriptions appear to the same, or worse Disadvantage, to others. But here it may be objected, why then do you send your Poem into the World?—— I'm really puzzled what answer to make.——Why— 'twas— because,— and this, and t'other Thing.—— Now I have it ! 'twas because an old Proverb says, Better late than never; and if this Reason is not found as convincing as any Demonstration in Euclid, I pronounce that whoever thinks otherwise, has not even the Shadow of Reason in Him.

But

PREFACE.

But not to trifle on so very serious and important an Occasion. I expect that the Conduct of the Poem will be thought wild and irregular, and consequently that it will be declar'd no Imitation, in that respect, of the Particulars it pretends to describe; since not the least Confusion, no motely Mixture of Persons of the most opposite Ranks and Conditions; no crouding, no obstreperous Tatling, were seen, felt, heard, or understood, in the Place abovemention'd.——— I in Truth am so conscious of the Justness of this Criticism, that I blush to think of it: And to whisper a Word in the Reader's Ear, I endeavour'd to mend it, but found that every part of the Poem in question, might so justly be made or Head, or Middle or Tail, that there was no Possibility of my disposing it to better Advantage than that in which it now ventures abroad.

Some Persons of uncommon Penetration and Taste, who, very wisely, are for subjecting a'l kinds of Poetry to the Laws of the Drama, declare, that I have been guilty of a great Indecorum, in setting Hannah *the Water-Nymph in so conspicuous a Light,*

and

PREFACE.

*and in making her even eclipse several great
Ladies.—— Notwithstanding the prodigious
Strength of this Criticism, I yet shall come
off with flying Colours; for I have only imitated, in this Particular, the greatest comic
Genius this Age or Nation, or indeed any
other, has produc'd; I mean the Author of
the R. M. the Servants in which wonderful
Play (as full oft is seen in real Life) make
a much more considerable Figure than their
Masters.— If this Authority does not silence
the most prying, inveterate Critick, —qu'il
s'en aille.——*

*Firmly persuaded I am, that the ever-
lasting Return of the Word* Dis-habille, *will
administer uncommon Titillation and Delight to a musical Ear. Now tho' I probably
may be thought an* ORIGINAL *in this kind of
Chiming, I yet will be so ingenuous as to
confess (for I abominate any thing which
has the Air of Plagiarism) that many Poets of our own, and of some other polite
and learned Nations, had got the Start of
me in this Species of Harmony. I believe
the late delectable Mr.* Thomas Durfey *of
Sing-song Memory, might very naturally be*
                                              cited

cited on this Occasion. The bare mention of this charming Creature raises me to Extasy. Peace to his Ashes! Never sure will so sweet a Warbler arise again, of which his Trillos, Twangdillos, and their numerous Progeny, are an immortal Proof.

But I am going to make my Entry larger than my House, so shall hardly have room (observe the Pun) for any thing else.—— With regard, therefore, to the other Pieces, they were writ as the Fit of—— I know not what to call it, came upon me. Possibly a Query will be made, why I publish so many Fragments, and not the entire Poems from which they are extracted: But here again I have a most substantial Reason. Modern Poesies (Noverint universi per præsentes) are of so light and subtle a Nature, that they frequently evaporate, in their Conveyance from the Author's Brain (if he has any) to the Paper, and from thence to the Press. Now when this happens to Poems of a considerable Length, 'tis manifest that the honest Bibliopole stands but a sort of a very poor Chance.

Of

PREFACE.

Of my Imitations I shall say very little. I certainly look upon'em (with the most profound Modesty I speak this) as infinitely superior to the Originals, from which they are taken, otherwise should not have been so silly as to print them Face to Face. A Word or two more will finish this very short Preamble. As the first Importer of any rare or useful Commodity is had in Esteem upon that Account, I very justly expect that some regard should be paid to me, inasmuch as I James Drake am the first Englishman who has transfus'd Chinese and Gascoon Poetry into his native Language.

A Manuscript Ode of Mr. de Voltaire having fallen accidentally into my Hands, I thought proper to communicate it to the Publick.

ERRATA.

CON-

CONTENTS.

Kifs

CONTENTS.

THE

THE

HUMOURS

OF

NEW TUNBRIDGE WELLS

AT

ISLINGTON.

WHENCE comes it that the fhining Great,

To Titles born, and awful State,

Thus condefcend, thus check their Will,

And fcud away to *Tunbridge Wells,*

To mix with vulgar Beaux and Belles?

Ye Sages your fam'd Glaffes raife,

Survey this Meteor's dazling Blaze,

And fay, portends it Good or Ill.

B   Soon

Soon as Aurora gilds the Skies,

With brighter Charms the Ladies rife,

 To dart forth Beams that fave or kill.

No Homage at the Toilette paid,

(Their lovely Features unfurvey'd,)

Sweet Negligence her Influence lends,

And all the artlefs Graces blends,

 That form the tempting Dishabille.

Behold the Walks, a chequer'd Shade,

In the gay Pride of Green array'd:

 How bright the Sun! the Air how ftill!

In wild Confufion there we view

 Red Ribbons groop'd with Aprons blue.

Scrapes, Curtzies, Nods, Winks, Smiles and Frowns;

Lords, Milkmaids, Dutcheffes and Clowns,

 In their all-various Dishabille.

       Thus,

Thus, in the famous Age of Gold,

(Not quite romantic tho' fo old)

 Mankind were merely *Jack* and *Gill.*

On flow'ry Banks, by murm'ring Streams,

They tatled, walk'd, had pleafing Dreams,

But drefs'd indeed, like aukward Folks;

No Steeple-Hats, Surtouts, fhort Cloaks,

 Fig-leaves the only Dishabille.——

Sudden a clatt'ring Shower defcends,

A ruftling's heard, the Strolling ends,

 And foon the Breakfaft-Rooms now fill.

Like Bees faft-flocking to their Hive,

Men, Women, all, fkim, pufh and drive:

The Chairs (firft come, firft ferv'd) they feize,

No Spark cries, *Madam*, ——*This*, ——*nay Pleafe*:——

 Their Manners in high Dishabille.

      Swift

Swift clears the Sky, the Crouds difperfe,

Another Scene adorns my Verfe,

    Parties who modifh Liquids fwill.

Prefto, before our famifh'd Eyes,

Mountains of Bread and Butter rife.

Smart *Ganymedes* wait round in Throngs,

And yet, alas! no Napkins, Tongs,

    The Equipage in Dishabille.

Silence! for *(a)* Sir *Cockade* appears,

To Angel-Sounds prepare your Ears,

    He hums *the Lafs of Patie's Mill*:

Then trips a Minuet round the Floor

(Such Steps no Mortal faw before!)

Sits, ftarts, peers, lolls, twirls *Royal Jack*;

Aims at a Caper, flounces back,

    His Brain in gay, mad Dishabille.

What

What *(b)* Fair-One there draws ev'ry Eye?

Around her, Thousands, giggling, fly——

She speaks in Accents faintly shrill.

" *I in a Pr——nce's Smiles am blest;*

" *That you are not.* ——*Now where's the Jest?*

Alas! those Prudes who most deride,

Wou'd, were *(c)* *Ithuriel's* Spear apply'd,

Trip back in more than Dishabille.

Ye Maids who genuine Maidens are,

Of gaudy, flutt'ring Sparks beware,

Who vain, gay, luscious Thoughts instil.

For shou'd you, charm'd by Plumes and Lace,

(Too often these extinguish Grace)

Withdraw to unfrequented Bow'rs,

A Snake, swift-gliding from the Flowers,

Wou'd ruffle all your Dishabille.

B 3   Who's

Who's that illumes the middle Path?

Immortal *N—ſh*, dread King of *Bath*,

   Great Soul of Hazard, Whiſk, Quadrille.

He forms in his capacious Mind,

Bright Schemes to poliſh all Mankind :

Balls, Concerts, Scandal, Modes, Intrigues ;

Joins with the Rich in glorious Leagues,

   And Nicks—— their very Dishabille.

How bright's the Blaze round yonder Groop?

The firſt of that illuſtrious Troop,

   Is Who? The *(d)* Sage that boaſts his Pill.

" *Osford*, he cries, *ſhall 'ave my Sone,*

' *So Cambreege, Zeſt! is al ondone.*"

Superbe he treats Duke, Lord or Knight :

Bleſt Pills! thus high to raiſe a Wight,

   From a pedantic Dishabille.

I dream

I dream, or rosy Cupids sport,

Sure Beauty's Queen here keeps her Court,

  Such mingled Charms the Senses thrill.

But *(e) Chloe* comes! they fade, they die;

Like Light she flashes on the Eye.

Thus tempting, gay *Thalestris* won

The Heart of *Philip*'s mighty Son,

  In her Equestrian Dishabille.

Inchanted with her ev'ry Grace,

Swift through the Grove her Steps I trace,

  She's gone! I feel a deadly Chill.

In deep Despair I gaze around,

Ah me! no heavenly Fair is found.

Restore Her, *Morpheus*, or I die;

Blest Vision chear my longing Eye,——

  But O! without the Dishabille.

The

The Flag's display'd, the Cannon fire, *(f)*

To nobler Sounds I wind the Lyre,

   The Echoes reach the distant Hill.

Lo' from their Car three Nymphs descend,

The Zephyrs, Sports and Loves attend,

Whose Bosoms heaving with Delight,

Think the three *Graces* bless their Sight,

   For once veil'd in a Dishabille.

Lovely Mistake! for *Brunswick's* Face,

We, in their shining Features trace,

   Their seraph Smiles our Vows fulfil.

Thus Deities in antient Times,

(Or Bards fib soundly in their Rhimes)

To glad poor Mortals, left the Skies,

Wrapt in the airy, bright Disguise

   Of a celestial Dishabille.

In

In yon Alcove *Monimia* lies;

A Youth attracted by her Sighs,

   Steals to the lovely Dreamer——till

Soft whisp'ring in an amorous Strain,

The Fair, in Sleep, reveals her Pain.

Ah! fond *Monimia*'s felf betray'd,——

Twas to her Charmer fhe difplay'd

   Her Soul in Love-fick Dishabille.

Again my *Chloe*! yes! 'tis She!

She fhines! She's gone! ftill wretched Me!

   O for a *Kneller*, and *(g) Paul Brill!*

Or could'ft thou, *(h) Philips*, catch her Charms,

The rofeat Smile, the Glance that warms;

Paint her, foft-flumbring in a Glade,

I'd fly to clafp the Magic Shade,

   And kifs away the Dishabille.

Stand

Stand clear ! for now a motley Crew

Pours like a Flood from Midnight Stew ;

    Light-finger'd Knaves who Pockets drill ;

Wits, Captains, Politicians, Trulls;

Sots, Devotees, Pimps, Poets, Gulls ;

And Jews, who breathing lecherous Sighs,

Drink Chriſtian Beauty at their Eyes

    That dart quite through the Dishabille.

To me, *(i) Sophronia,* gives a Glaſs :

Cries, —Fill it, Bard : —with Glee I'd paſs

    Inſtant to the ſalubrious Rill ;

When oh ! by Hoops contiguous preſt,

My Heart faſt-flutters in my Breaſt ;

The Cauſe ſweet *Sympathy* reveals ;——

Cupids unnumber'd She conceals

    Beneath the circling Dishabille.

Got

Got to the Rails, with as much Eaſe

As Merit into Courts can ſqueeze,

   I cry— O *(k) Hannah!* thou Junquil ;

By the dear Zone that binds thy Leg,

One cool, vivific Glaſs I beg !

'Tis for a Matron, in Deſpair,

Unleſs theſe Waters give an Heir ;

   Her Soul in Spleen's dark Dishabille.

Yet *Hannah,* deaf to all my Cries,

Throws fliggering round her Sky-blue Eyes.——

   Thou charming Naïad, ſee ! I grill.——

Ah me ! my Dreſs, my Bard-like Air,

Tell her— too plain— No Rhino's there.——

Grand Ladies thus, (their Porters too)

When trembling Scribes for Favours ſue,

   Like Winds, ſport with their Dishabille,

6   But

But now the Naiad hears my Sighs,

She hands a Glafs, too fleeting Prize!

   For O Reverfe! each drop I fpill.

Sad Emblem!— Once to *Gr——f——n's* Grace

I flew—— not for the *Laureat's* Place:

Gay rofe my Hopes, as *Phœbus* bright,

A moment blaz'd, then plung'd in Night,

   And all was worfe than Dishabille.——

It glows: On Flowers I fall to reft;

Come *Zephyr*, come, and fan my Breaft,

   Or in cool, pearly Drops diftill.

Muft I again to Town return,

And 'midft its fultry Ardors burn!

I'll hafte to fome fequeftred Place;

Ah no! for *Fortune* fhows a Face

   Still frowning, and all Dishabille

                    And

And yet, wou'd gracious *Hartford* praise,

In echoing Shades my Voice I'd raise,

   Or down by Rivulets sweetly trill.

I'd wander 'midst the spangled Dews,

And Nature's spacious Book peruse :

At Court outshine great *Duck* himself,

Not dangling creep, a shiv'ring Elf,

   In my poetic Dishabille.

What's Reputation? oft a Blaze,

That throws, (but with fictitious Rays,)

   A Glory round the meanest Quill.

Ev'n in that shadowy Lustre drest;

My Muse may please and be carest ;

May Splendois dart shall charm the Croud,

So grow of fancied Beauties proud,

   Tho' homely and in Dishabille.

                (a) Mr

(a) Mr Mart—n, by some call'd the Tunbridge Knight, an inoffensive Gentleman, known chiefly by the yellow Cockade in his Hat, and the Hawk he carried upon his Fist He gave the Name of ROYAL JACK to that Bird, out of Respect, as he said, to the Royal Family

(b) The honourable Miss V————e, who met with very rude treatment in this Place

(c) Alluding to the Spear of that Angel in the Paradise lost

(d) Dr M a sort of Physician, fam'd for his Pills, but much more for his Genius and Learning This great Man being refus'd his Doctor's Degree at Cambridge, vow'd, with a noble Indignation, he'd ruin that University —— His Son shou'd go to Oxford

(e) The Honourable Miss H———— in a riding Habit

(f) The Princesses had always this Honour paid them, at their Arrival in the Walks

(g) A famous Landskip Painter.

(h) Mr Philips junior, Painter in Great Queen street, Lincoln's-Inn Fields

(i) The celebrated Lady Sar

(k) The Wench which serv'd the Water at the Well

The

The Miftake, or St. *James*'s Palace, and
the new Stables in the *Meufe*.

A Stranger gazing on the Stables, cries,

With Air auguft, thefe royal Manfions rife;

Spying, anon, St. *James's* aukward Pile,

Really, fays he, thefe Stables graçe the Ifle.——

Convinc'd that inftant of his grofs Miftake,

Enrag'd, thefe Words like Lightning from him break;

Full worthy this of *Houynhymns* and Brutes,

But meanly with the *Britifh* Genius fuits.——

Say, wav'ring Nation, whence this Caprice fprings,

Kings lodg'd as Horfes, and as Horfes, Kings?

The

The Author's WISH.

From a Manuscript Lyric Poem, entitled,
The Complaint, to his Genius.

NOT that Ambition me seduc'd,

 To soar on Fortune's painted Wing:

Far humbler Motives, strong induc'd,

 To haunt, unvex'd, the Muses Spring.

Some rural Cott, where Angel-Peace,

 Mild o'er the Soul her Influence sheds;

Where Pleasures flow with gay Increase,

 And sport at ease on rosy Beds.

Where Sylvan Scenes the Fancy raise,

 Exalt the Soul, improve the Lay;

Where

Where fanning Zephyrs footh the Blaze

    Of Summer's fiercely-darting Day.

Here doubly bleft, devoid of Care,

    The circling Hours fhould blifsful flide;

No gilded Views my Soul enfnare,

    The Ivy wreathe my only Pride.

The dimpled Stream, the winding Shade,

    The Lawn in chearing Verdure dreft;

Th' afpiring Hill, the tufted Glade,

    Soft Themes' fhou'd pleafing Thoughts fuggeft.

Then rais'd to Extafy, I'd hail

    The fweetly-awful rural Powers;

Invite, if artlefs Sounds prevail,

    Gay Wood-Nymphs from their Jafmin Bowers.

Rich

Rich in my felf I'd frown on Gold;

 And far the treacherous Gugaw throw;

With Pity's melting Eye behold,

 The idly-buftling Croud below.——

Ah me! in what romantic Seats,

 Does my deluded Fancy ftray:

Too tranfient, vifionary Sweets,

 That fudden gleam, then fade away.

Thus, fportive, to the Mind, in Sleep,

 Cafcades, Rocks, Coaches, Guineas rife;

Break but the Charm, the glitt'ring Heap,

 And all the wild Creation dies.

Th

The Experienc'd MATRON.

FOUR modish Dames, not prone to Ill,

Were playing at their dear Quadrille:

Swift whisk'd the Cards, and *Fortune* flew

From Side to Side, as Courtiers do.——

This Fair, one Moment's flush'd with Joy,

The next, her brightest Hopes destroy:

The Play, their Humours soon betray'd,

And Smiles and Frowns alternate play'd.

Now *Betty* handed round the Tea,

And crown'd the Feast with Ratafia.——

Rap goes the Door: the Ladies' start:——

Says *Chloe*,—— 'tis my *Drake!* my Heart!

Your Husband!—— Pugh—— 'tis Captain *Plume*:——

The Captain!—— So!—— and He's at *Rome.*——

I'd

I'd e'en have giv'n my Fancy Scope,

And told us, 'twas,—Pray who?—The Pope.

This rais'd a Laugh, the Fans are spread——

Rap, rap—— Fly *Betty!* sure you're dead!——

One vow'd 'twas *Squib*, another *Rake*,

But all insisted 'twas'nt *Drake*.

When *Chloe*, redning with a Grace,

That wak'd new Beauties in her Face;

Cries—— What d'ye take me for?—— a Stock——

Who best shou'd know my Spouse's *Knock?*

From a Manuscript Poem, entitled, *The Progress of Learning.*

BE it, O Science! radiant Maid,
   To thy immortal Honour told,

That whilst thy heavenly Dictates sway'd,

   Fair *Virtue* triumph'd over Gold.

4   But

But when thy Smiles no more cou'd charm,

 And *Romans* flighted thy Embrace,

Vice blazon'd forth her painted Form,

 And weeping *Virtue* left the Place.

Then down finks thy devoted Head,

 And *Vandals* to complete thy Doom,

Wide o'er the World dire Havock fpread,

 Thy Fanes deftroy, and all is Gloom.

Paft fome few Years, a fhapelefs Sprite,

 Offspring of Cloyfters ap'd thy Mien:

Glanc'd aukward, thro' the fullen Night,

 And faintly cheer'd the widow'd Scene.——

Sudden the fcatter'd Vapours fly

 To Realms where Midnight Darknefs reigns;

For

For lo! the genial Blaze is nigh,

    That gilds once more *Ausonia's* Plains.

Tis come! for (a) *Leo* mounts the Throne,

    Neglected Art's auspicious Friend;

The golden Years his Influence own,

    And raptur'd Joys his Steps attend.

Had every Pontiff smil'd like thee

    On Learning's Sons, and sooth'd their Flame,

Rome still o'er all wou'd Mistress be,

    And justly boast the glorious Name.

(a) Pope *Leo* x.

From

From a Manuscript Poem, entitled,
The Progress of Poetry.

WHEN *Grecians* liv'd, auspicious Time!

Glory inspir'd the sacred Rage:

How faint the Muse of *Albion*'s Clime,

Now glimmers in th'enervate Page!

Then Sculpture wak'd the mimic Stone,

With Nature's Tints the Canvas glow'd,

Sad *Orpheus* breath'd melodious Moan,

And *Clio* taught the sounding Ode.

Blest Period! fairest point of Time,

Th' enraptur'd Muses golden Age,

When Arts that rais'd their Heads sublime,

With genial Warmth inspir'd the Sage:

C 4   No

No grov'ling Views cou'd then controul

The Sage's high exalted Guſt;

Once fir'd, he'd fly from Pole to Pole,

To ſlake his nobly-ardent Thirſt.

So to the radiant Source of Light,

Allur'd by the refulgent Blaze,

Jove's Bird directs his rapid Flight,

And on the God does ſtedfaſt gaze.

Grandeur was then of mild Acceſs,

No (b) Cerberus held faſt the Door;

Nor Worth, tho' in a pining Dreſs,

The Marks of wild Dejection wore.

(b) Alluding to great Mens Porters.

To

To Solitudes in vain the Muſe

    Fled baſhful, pleas'd with calm Reſorts ;

Fame, ſwift as Light, her Steps purſues,

    And calls her forth to ſhine in Courts.

Thus gay *Anacreon*'s melting Lyre,

    On which the Loves enamour'd hung,

Soft eccho'd to th' *Athenian* Choir,

    And *Ios* hail'd the Poet's Song.

Athens' mild *(c)* Chief, for Arts renown'd,

    Indulg'd the Bard a fav'rite Smile;

Struck with the Harp's harmonious Sound,

    He call'd him ſoon from *Teos*' Iſle.

(c) *Hipparchus*

Seeing

Seeing his Daughter (an Infant) in her
Coffin.

SEE! where she lies, in baleful Weeds array'd,

(The Tribute Heaven requires so early paid)

Who, call a Moment back, in flow'ry Pride,

Seem'd, in her Ribbons gay, an infant Bride.

With Rapture then I gaz'd upon thy Charms,

And clasp'd Thee, sweetly smiling, in my Arms;

Saw fondest Joys in distant Prospect rise,

When thou, in Years advanc'd, shou'dst glad these

Eyes.

How false those Joys! (so promising the Theme)

On airy Pinions gliding like a Dream,

For lo! Death's icy Hand has chill'd her Veins,

And snatch d, relentless, to his dread Domains,——

Yet

Yet no !— the blushing Graces in her Cheek,

Her Lips, like Roses red, which all but speak;

The Smiles that round her opening Features gleam,

Display the Virgin in a pleasing Dream.

Some guardian Seraph in his silent Round,

Thee beauteous as his kindred Angels found;

In heavenly Slumbers, soft, thine Eyelids prest,

And soon he'll wing thee to eternal Rest.

EPIGRAM.

I'VE but one Wife, says *Hodge*, and She,
  A more than Vixon proves to me——
But how liv'd Men in Days of Yore,
When each was plagu'd with half a score!

EPIGRAM.

MOPSA whipping her Scarf on, scuds away
to the Park,

And cries, for a Venus I'll pass in the dark.

With her Hoop spreading wide, and her soft-
soothing Tale,

She knows her coarse Features may sometimes prevail.

Well, the Baggage plays arch, thus to wound in
the Night,

Since her Face wou'd strike Dread, if reveal'd in the
Light.

To

To One who inveigh'd very much againſt
the few Things that were judg'd toler-
able, but applauded all the trifling Particulars, in a dramatic Piece of the Author's, not yet exhibited.

E P I G R A M.

GUſtillo, with a witleſs Face,
Damns ev'ry Stroke that aims at Grace,

But praiſes each mean Thought or Word.

Thus Flies, begot in ſtupid Stinks,

Leaving the Vi'lets, Roſes, Pinks,

Buzz round, and ſettle on a————

Upon Mrs. *Cecilia Young*'s representing
Britannia, in the Opera so call'd.

NO more shall *Italy* its Warblers send,

To charm our Ears with *Handel*'s hea-

venly Strains;

For dumb his (*d*) rapt'rous Lyre, their Fame must end,

And lo! *Cecilia* from th' Ætherial Plains:

Her Voice once call'd an Angel from the Skies,

To sing like Accents, see! she hither flies.

(*d*) At the time that *Britannia* was represented, the Opera of *Cato,*
(not compos'd by Mr *Handel*) was playing at the Theatre Royal in the
Hay-Market.

The

The jealous Shepherdefs.

S O N G.

Imitated from *la Fontaine's Fables.*

SWEET *Amaryllis*, blooming Fair,
  By Love reduc'd to fad Defpair,

Sufpecting gay *Myrtillo's* Truth,

Reproach'd in Wilds the abfent Youth,

Thinking her Sheep, and Dog alone,

Cou'd hear her breathe this Love-fick Moan.

But *Celadon* who fpied the Maid,

Steals to the Willow's fecret Shade;

Thence hears her recommend her Sighs

To *Zephyrus*, and as he flies,

To tell her perjur'd Swain—— She dies.

Women

Women like Books.

SONG.

The Tune, *As Cupid one Day wily*, &c.

A Girl we long to toy with,

   Is like a favourite Book;

If once we're ſet agog on't,

   We long to ſteal a Look.

Tranſported with the Notion

   Of Bliſs that ne'er will cloy,

So ſwift we whiſk it over,'

   We taſte no real Joy.

But when the Rapture's ended,

   And coolly we peruſe,

The Pleaſure is ſubſtantial,

   And ſooths our fondeſt Views.   Then

Then once, twice, thrice, we thumb it,

Perhaps five hundred times;

At laft it grows infipid,

As *(a) Colley's* annual Rhimes.

(a) At the fame time that our Author is fo ludicrous upon this Gentleman, he is fenfible how much he has excelled in another Species of Writing.

A SONG.

The Tune.

The Night her blackeſt Sables wore, &c.

CAN any Tranſports equal thoſe
  Which two fond Lovers feel,
Who meet, that thought to meet no more,
  And their paſt Woes reveal.

Their Joys too great to be expreſs'd,
  So croud the faultring Tongue,
Fain would they breathe their Soul in Words,
  But Paſſion ſtrikes them dumb.

Yet do their Eyes at the bleſt Sight,
  Enraptur'd Glances dart,
By theſe and Sighs their Wiſhes paint,
  Which flutter round the Heart.

Like

Like Statues fix'd, amaz'd they ſtand,

Survey their mutual Charms;

Then, when the Extaſy gives leave,

Fly to each other's Arms.

SONG

SONG.

The Tune, *Fike of Dunkrab.*

A Painter draws a homely Coquet,

    Who charg'd him ſtrictly not to flatter:

Miſs her Likeneſs views, but frets,

    And cries, O Heavens! the Satyr.

He takes his Bruſh,— daſh out goes the Face,

    He paints a lovely, finiſh'd Creature:

Now Miſs peeps,— ſays She, here's Grace,

    'Tis me in ev'ry Feature.

The Fond Difappointment.

S O N G.

Set to Mufick by the honourable Col——

LUCY, bright Nymph, who long had frown'd,
    To all my amorous Glances blind,
At laft, my conftant Paffion crown'd,
    And now, as Love cou'd wifh, was kind.

I clafp'd the Charmer to my Heart,
    Inchanted with her fnowy Frame;
The fweet Illufion made me ftart,
    I wak'd—— for Oh! 'twas but a Dream.

Le Cadenat.

Par Mr. *de Voltaire.*

JEUNE *Beauté qui ne savés que plaire,*

    A vos genoux comme bien vous savés,

En qualité de Prêtre de Cythere,

J'ai débité non morale sévere,

Mais bien sermons par Venus approuvez,

Gentils propos, & toutes les sornettes,

Dont Rochebrune orne ses Chansonnettes.

De ces sermons votre Cœur fut touché,

Jurates lors de quitter le peché

Que parmi nous on nomme indifference:

Plus

The *Italian* Padlock.

Imitated from Mr. *de Voltaire*.

GAY, blooming *Chloe*, form'd to pleafe,
How often, on my bended Knees,

Have I, bright *Venus* Prieft, to You,

Read moral Lectures, tender, new ;

Not dry, fevere, infipid Strains,

But fuch as Beauty's Queen ordains ;

Soft-foothing Words, inveigling Praife,

Borrow'd from *Prior*'s melting Lays ?

Deep funk my Precepts in your Mind,

When you (to gentle Love refign'd)

The Sin, one balmy Hour, difclaim'd,

By am'rous Mortals Coldnefs nam'd ;

And

Plus un Baiser m'en donna l'aſſurance ;

Mais votre Epoux, ma mie, a tout gâté.

Il craint l'Amour.   Mari ſexagenaire

Contre ce Dieu fut toujours en colere,

C'eſt bien raiſon, l'Amour de ſon coté,

Aſſez ſouvent ne les épargne guere.

Celui ci donc tient de court vos appas.

Plus ne venez ſur les bords de la Seine,

Dans ces jardins où blondins à centaine,

En rendez-vous vont prendre leurs ébats,

Où tous les ſoirs Nymphes jeunes & blanches,

Les Courcillons, Polignacs, Ville-Franches,

Près du Baſſin devant plùs d'un Paris

De la beauté vont diſputer le prix.

And fweetly to increafe our Blifs

Seal'd the dear Promife with a Kifs,

But Oh! your Hufband, lovelieft Fair,

Has plung'd my Hopes in deep Defpair.

Cupid he dreads; for Spoufes, who,

Have fpun out Life to fixty two,

Deteft the God of rofy Smiles:——

Juftly—— for Cupid oft beguiles

Antique fond Hufbands with his Wiles.

This Churl my *Chloe*'s Charms immures,

And like a precious Gem fecures.

No more on *Thames'* green Banks you walk,

Shed Angel Smiles, and fweetly talk

Amid the Choirs of noble Maids,

Who brighten *Ham*'s delicious Shades,

Bleft

Plus ne venez au Palais des * Francines,

Dans ce païs où tout est fiction,

Où l'Amour seul fait mouvoir cent machines,

Plaindre Thésée & siffler Arion.

Trop bien helas ! à votre époux soumise,

On ne vous voit tout au plus qu'a l'Eglise.

Le scelerat a de plus attenté

Par cas nouveau fur votre liberté.

* L'Opera

Pour

Bleſt Shades! where *Richmond* leads the Train

Of Graces who adorn her Reign.

No more in *(a)* Lyric Shews you ſhine,

Where all is Fiction, all Divine :

Soft Seats! where *Love* the Scepter-ſways ;

Himſelf, Machines unnumber'd plays ;

Draws Tears for fair *(b) Amelia*'s Doom,

Or lights fierce *(c) Judith* to her Tomb.

For oh! ſubjected to your Spouſe,

And curſt by Hymeneal Vows,

To Church you only now repair,

And Spouſee dangles with You there.——

Still this might paſs, had not the Wretch,

Employ'd, alas! a wicked Fetch ;

(a) The Opera   (b) An Opera ſet by Mr *Lampe*
(c) An *Oratorio*, play'd but once.

A Fetch

Pour éclaircir pleinement ce myftere,

D'un peu plus haut reprenons notre affaire.

Vous connoiſſez la Déeſſe Cérès :

Or en ſon temps Cérès eut une fille,

Semblable à vous à vos ſcrupules près,

Belle & ſenſible, honneur de ſa famille,

Brune ſurtout, partant pleine d'attraits,

Ain

A Fetch was hinted to the Dunce,

Excludes dear Gallantry at once.——

How hard, my *Chloe*, is your Cafe!

Yet! but with Sighs, I'll dare to trace

The Origin of this Difgrace.

Of *Ceres* frequently you've read,

Who fhar'd the mighty Thund'rer's Bed.

From their Embrace a Daughter fprung

Whofe Beauties raptur'd Bards have fung.

Your Heavenly Frame in her's was feen,

The piercing Glance, the dazling Mein;

Like you, the Glory of her Race,

To Softnefs form'd, and fweeteft Grace;

A bright Brunette, and therefore bleft

With ev'ry Charm by Nymphs poffeft;

In

Ainsi que vous par le Dieu d'Hymenée,

La pauvre enfant fut assez mal menée.

Le Roi des Morts fut son barbare Epoux,

Il étoit louche, avare, hargneux, jaloux ;

Il fut Cocu, c'etoit bien la justice.

Pirithoüs son fortuné rival,

In fhort, were *Chloe* lefs fevere,

The juft Refemblance of my Dear.

Proferpina, this Pearl of Maids

Was call'd, in *Pluto*'s dreary Shades.

Her fquinting Confort, like to yours,

Was vers'd in Woman's artful Lures,

So *Hymen* made this beauteous Wife,

Like *Chloe* lead a difmal Life:

For *Pluto*, fordid, jealous, fower,

Clofe watch'd her in his gloomy Bower:

And how did fhe reward her Spoufe?

With Horns, the Fair-One, grac'd his Brows.

You know *Pirithoüs*, vent'rous Blade,

To Hell, by fecret Paths, had ftray'd.

Polite,

Beau, jeune, adroit, complaisant, liberal,

Au Dieu Pluton donna le Benefice

De Cocuage , or ne demandez pas,

Comment un homme avant sa derniere heure,

Put penétrer en la sombre demeure.

Cet homme aimoit, l'Amour guidoit ses pas.

Mais aux Enfers comme aux lieux où vous êtes,

Voiez qu'il est peu d'intrigues secretes.

De sa chaudiere un damné d'Espion

Vit ce grand cas, & dit tout à Pluton.

Polite, gay, generous and young,

He charm'd her with his——*flowing Tongue*;

The sweet Infection reach'd her Heart,

And hence the sable Monarch's Smart,

His dark Ideas, barbarous Schemes,

And Rivals tort'ring, even in Dreams.——

Now ask not how a Mortal born,

(Before his last, sad Hour was drawn)

Cou'd visit *Pluto*'s beauteous Bride;

He lov'd—— and *Cupid* was his Guide.

But most Intrigues are blabb'd in Hell,

As zealously as where we dwell.

From his deep Cauldron where he fried,

A Fiend the dallying Couple spied;

E

He·

Le dieu donna sa Femme à tous les Diables.

Premiers transports sont un peu pardonnables.

Bien tot après devant son Tribunal,

Il convoqua le senat infernal,

A son conseil viennent les noires ames,

De ces maris dévolus aux enfers,

Qui dès long-tems en cocuage experts,

Pendant leur vie ont tourmenté leurs femmes.

Un

He haſtes to the tremendous King,

And cries, I've ſeen a—— monſtrous Thing.——

He tells him all—— the Monarch flies

Swift as a Whirlwind thro' the Skies,

And ſorely he his Queen abus'd,

(Firſt Starts of Rage may be excus'd)

Then, wiſh'd her Gig (in Terms uncivil)

Demoliſh'd by the uglieſt Devil.——

Quite frantic grown, he ſummons all

His Senate, to their ſpacious Hall,

When ſtrait the ſooty Souls repair

Of Huſbands; All were Cuckolds there;

All vers'd in Jealouſy's dark Arts,

Thoſe Peſts to Wives—— of tender Hearts.

Loud

Un d'eux lui dit, mon confrere & seigneur,

Pour détourner la maligne influence,

Dont votre Altesse a fait l'experience,

Occir sa femme est toujours le meilleur;

Mais las! seigneur, la vôtre est immortelle.

Je voudrois donc pour votre sûreté,

Qu'un Cadenat de Structure nouvelle

Fût le garand de sa fidelité.

A la vertu par la force asservie,

Lors vos plaisirs borner ont son envie,

Plus ne sera d'Amant favorisé,

Et plût aux Dieux, que quand j'etois en vie

D'un tel secret je me fusse avisé!

Loud fpeaks a Shade— my Brother, Liege,

To crufh the Woes your Brain Befiege,

You'd beft— ftay— yes— difpatch your Wife,

But oh! She boafts immortal Life.

Wou'd therefore, to fecure the Dame,

Some Artift a Machine cou'd frame,

Of Structure new, a Mafterpiece,

That might enfure your future Peace,

By locking faft a private Door,

Which has fo plagu'd You heretofore.—

Then forc'd to tread fair Virtue's round,

Your Will wou'd all her Pleafures bound;

In vain Gallants wou'd whine and flatter,—

Since never, never they'd come at Her.—

Wou'd Heavens! I'd known, in Days of yore,

This Artifice.— I fay no more.

The

A ce Difcours les Diables applaudirent,

Et fur l'airain les Cocus l'ecrivirent.

En un moment fers, enclumes, fourneaux,

Sont preparez aux gouffres infernaux.

Tifiphoné de ces Lieux ferruriere,

Au Caderat met la main la premiere:

Elle

The Devils fmil'd at this Harangue,

And the high Arch with Plaudits rang.

Each Cuckold, wife as *Sancho's* Afs,

Engrav'd it on eternal Brafs.

Swift, Forges, Hammers, Anvils, Bars,

A fkilful *Cyclop*-Fiend prepares.

Tifiphone, in *Vulcan's* ftead,

Tortures the Steel, now flaming red:

She throws it into thoufand Shapes,

And ftill the Form defir'd efcapes,

At laft fhe cries— I have it right,

When lo! a PADLOCK rofe to Sight.

To its Succefs all largely Quaff,

And *Vulcan* roar'd a horrid Laugh.

Soon

Elle l'acheve ; & des mains de Pluton,

Proferpina reçoit le trifte don.

On m'a conté qu'effayant fon ouvrage,

Le cruel Dieu fut ému de pitié,

Qu' avec tendreffe il dit à fa moitié,

Que je vous plains ! vous allez être fage.

Or ce fecret aux enfers inventé,

Chez les humains tôt après fut porté,

Et

Soon raptur'd *Pluto* grasps the Prize,

And to his sorrowing Partner flies.

She takes the fatal Gift, she swoons;

A gushing Flood her Beauty drowns.——

I'm told the surly God confest,

Compassion warm'd his savage Breast,

As o'er her Form his Fingers stray'd,

When He, the curst Machine essay'd.

How much, he cried, I pity you!

To stollen Joys, hence, bid adieu.

'Tis done—— and now you must be true.

From Hell's black Realms this Secret brought,

Was soon to prying Mortals taught;

Since that, in *Rome*, as Trav'lers write,

There's not a Count, Citt, Pedant, Knight,

But

Et depuis ce, dans Venise & dans Rome,

Il n'est Pedant, Bourgeois, ni Gentilhomme,

Qui pour garder l'honneur de sa maison,

De Cadenats n'ait sa provision.

Là tout jaloux, sans crainte qu'on le blâme,

Met sous la clef la vertu de sa femme;

Or votre Epoux dans Rome a frequenté,

Chez les méchans on se gâte sans peine,

Et le galant est fort à la Romaine.

Mais ne craignez pour votre liberté,

Tous ses efforts seront pures vetilles.

Et mon Amour est plus fort mille fois,

Que Cadenats, verroux, portes, ni grilles.

But Padlocks has, a copious Store,

To keep Dishonour from his Door.

There, every Man, whose jealous Brain

With Rivals teems, (a dreaded Train)

May, fearless of, or sneer or blame,

Lock up the Virtue of his Dame.——

Now your gruff Sir has liv'd in *Rome*,

And hence my Dear may date her Doom,

For charm'd with that superbe Abode,

He worships every *Roman* Mode.——

Still, let not *Chloe* be dismay'd,

Nor weep her Liberty betray'd.

Soon *Venus* shall exert her Power,

And all your dearest Rights restore :

For O ! my Passion's stronger far,

Than Gate, Wall, Padlock, Bolt or Bar.

One

Le Baiser rendu.

Conte tiré de *la Fontaine*.

GUILLOT *paſſoit avec ſa Mariée.*

Un Gentilhomme à ſon gré la trouvant,

Qui t'a, dit-il, donné telle Epouſée?

Que je la baiſe, à la Charge d'autant.

Bien volontiers, dit Guillot à l'inſtant :

Elle eſt, Monſieur, fort à votre Service.

Le

Kifs for Kifs.

A TALE

Imitated from *La Fontaine*.

AS *Colin* faunter'd with his Bride,
A rural 'Squire the Couple fpied,
When tripping to 'em, *Col*, fays He,
This Beauty thine? It ne'er can be ——
Troth but She is, cries Lubber Lout;——
Then, quo' his Worfhip, turn about,
And let me kifs her Damafk Lip:
I muft; I will ·—— but juft a Sip.
When I am married, here's my Hand,
A Kifs fhall be at thy Command.

Nay, an 'tis fo, cries honeft *Col*,
You're welcome, fure, to bufs our *Doll*.

The

Le Monsieur donc fait alors son office

En appuyant ; Peronelle en rougit.

Huit jours après, ce Gentilhomme prit

Femme à son tour : à Guillot il permit

Même faveur.

Guillot

The 'Squire his eager Lips applies;

Quick to her Cheek the Colour flies——

Thank ye, fweet Sir—— away fhe hies.

But now his Worfhip, Folks declare,

Is wedded to a beauteous Fair.

Brifk *Colin* haftes, he fees the 'Squire,

The Lady comes, his Heart's on Fire.——

Quoth *Col* and grins—— Good Zir, I wot,

You have not yet your Word forgot:——

No, no:—— Why then I'll kifs the Dame.

He fmuggles, till fhe cries—— for Shame.

The

Guillot tout plein de zele,

Puisque, Monsieur, dit il, est si fidelle,

J'ai grand regret, & je suis bien faché,

Qu'ayant baisé seulement Peronelle,

Il n'ait encore avec elle couché.

The Clown retires with aukward Bow :——

A worthy Gentleman, I trow;

But when our *Dolly*'s Lips he prefs'd,

I wifh he'd carried on the Jeft;

For had they flipt between the Sheets,

O! I had tafted Honey Sweets!

Cupid

De Cupido & de sa Dame.

Tiré de *Marot*.

A Mour trouva celle qui m' est amere :

Et j'y estois, j'en sçay bien mieulx le compte :

Bon jour, dict il, bon jour Venus ma mere,

Puis tout à coup il veoit, qu'il se mescompte,

Dont la couleur au visage lui monte

The beautiful Miſtake.

Imitated from *Marot*.

A S *Mɪɪa* once and I were laid
Beneath the Woodbine's trembling Shade,

Comes Cupid——" Dear Mamma," he cries,

(Bright Anguiſh ſtealing from his Eyes)

" Alas! I've ſought You all the Day,

" Surpriz'd where my Mamma cou'd ſtray;

" O'er Dales, and Hills, and Rocks I flew,

" E'er gliding Fairies ſip the Dew:

" Sighing, to *Jove* I breath'd a Vow——

" 'Twas heard; for O! I've found You now "

Love's riſing Joy his Smiles expreſt,

When ſwift he ſprings to *Mɪɪa*'s Breaſt,

But going to kiſs her roſy Cheek,

Amaz'd he ſtarts, and ſcarce can ſpeak.

F 2 " Thus

D'avoir failly: honteux Dieu fçait combien:

Non, non, Amour, ce dy je, n'ayez honte:

Plus clers voyans que vous sy' trompent bien.

" Thus to miſtake ! O foul Diſgrace !"——

Confuſion ſweetly fluſh'd his Face——

" How Folks will laugh !"—— this wak'd his Pride ;

He hangs his Head, and turns aſide.

Seeing the *Rover* tortur'd thus ,

Fond Child, ſays I, why all this Fuſs ?

Suppreſs your Bluſhes, be not griev'd ;——

Much quicker Eyes have been deceiv'd.

From

Paſtor Fido. Atto I. Sce. IV.

COME *in vago giardin roſa gentile,*

Che ne le verdi ſue tenere ſpoglie

Pur dianzi era rinchiuſa ;

E ſotto l'ombra del notturno velo

Incolta, e ſconoſciuta

Stava peſando in ſul materno ſtelo ;

Al ſubito apparir del primo raggio

Che ſpunti in Oriente

Si deſta, e ſi riſente,

E ſcopre al ſol, che la vagheggia, e mira,

Il ſuo vermiglio & odorato ſeno,

Dov' Ape ſuſſurando

Ne i mattutini albori.

Vola fuggendo i rugiadoſi humori ;

Ma ſ'allor non ſi coglie,

From Scene IV. Act I.

Of *Paſtor Fido.*

The Virgin and the Roſe.

AS in ſome rural Paradiſe, a Roſe,

(Which, veil'd by Leaves, and huſh'd in

calm Repoſe,

Beneath the duſky Mantle of the Skies,

On its fair Stalk, in ſweet Oblivion lies)

Wakes gently, ſoon as the firſt Orient Beam

Calls ſlumb'ring Nature from its tranſient Dream:

To Phœbus, who its glowing Form beholds,

A Boſom, rich with Crimſon Hues, unfolds,

Whence the wing'd Bee, (ſoft-breathing amorous

Sighs)

Extracts the lucid Nectar as He flies.——

Bleſt

Sì che del mezzo dì senta le fiamme:

Cade al cader del sole

Sì scolorita in sù la siepe ombrosa,

Ch'à pena si può dir questa fù rosa.

Così la verginella,

Mentre cura materna

La custodisce, e chiude,

Chiude anch' ella il suo petto

A l'amoroso affetto:

Ma se lascivo sguardo

Di Cupido amator vien che la miri

E n' oda ella i sospiri,

Gli apre subito il core,

E nel tenero sen riceve amore.

Bleſt Flower! and yet if it ungather'd ſtay

Till Sol, high mounted, dart a ſcorching Ray,

Pining, it droops with the declining Light,

And all its Glories glide away from Sight.

Thus the young Virgin, whilſt her Mother's Care,

From flatt'ring Man conceals the darling Fair,

The Fair ſecludes Love's Ardours from her Breaſt,

And the ſoft Woes which break a Maiden's Reſt.

But ſhould ſome *Thyrſis* dart a wanton Eye,

And ſhe attend to the ſweet Tempter's Sigh,

Inſtant her Heart its inmoſt Folds diſplays,

And her, now Love-ſick Soul, is in a Blaze.

Then, if or Baſhfulneſs or Fear reſtrain

The melting Nymph, and ſhe diſguiſe her Pain,

E se vergogna il cela,

O temenza l'affrena,

La misera tacendo

Per soverchio desio tutta si strugge.

Così manca beltà, se'l foco dura,

E perdendo stagion, perde ventura.

To hated Silence doom'd, fhe weeping lies,

Eclips'd the lovely Luftre of her Eyes;

Her Graces fade, and fhe untimely dies.

SON-

SONNET.

Tiré des Oeuvres de Pièrre Goudelin,
Poëte Touloufain.

Hiér tant que le Caüs, le Chot, é la Cabéco

Trattaon à l'efcur de lours menuts afas,

E' que la trifto néyt-per mouftra fous lugras

Del gran calel del Cèl amagabo la méco.

Un Paftourél difio, b'é fayt uno grand péco

De douna moun amour à qui nou la bol pas,

A la bélo Liris, de qui l'armo de glas

Bol réndre pauromen ma perfuto buféco.

S O N N E T.

From *Goudelin*, a celebrated *Gafcoon* Poet.

Whilſt, ſhrouded by an Oak, in leafy State,

Two mutt'ring Owls were fix'd in grave

Debate,

(Slow, ſolemn Night, concealing Heav'n's bright Eye,

To ſhow her Train of Stars that gild the Sky.)

Poor *Colin*, ſighing :—— ſilly, ſure, he cries,

Am I to pine, ſince *Lucy* Love denies;

Coy *Lucy*, fair as Light, whoſe flinty Heart,

My Paſſion ſcorning, cauſes all my Smart.

How

Mentre que foun troupél rodo lè coumunal,

Yeu foun anat cent cops li parla de moun mal :

Més la cruélo cour à las autros Paftouros.

Ah! foulel de mous els, fè jamay fur toun fè

Yeu podi fourrupa dous poutets à plazé

Yeu farè ta gintet que duraren tres houros.

How oft, o'erwhelm'd with Grief, have I essay'd,

As, in the Primrose Dale, her Lambkins play'd,

To whisper Love? but still obdurate she,

Flew always, frowning, to the Nymphs from me.

Sun of my Eyes! as *Flora* sweetly gay,

Should once my Lips on thy soft Bosom stray,

Deliciously I'll raise the fragrant Bliss,

And feast three Hours upon a single Kiss.

Elogium * *Saulii, ex fabula quadam Sinica.*

VIX *ver incæperat cum Saulius flavum corticem Viridi pallio amiciret: pulchritudo ejus, pudore Suffundit mali Persici arborem, quæ, præ Indignatione flores, qui eam exornant, avellit atque in terram spargit. Splendor vivacissimorum colorum se non comparaverit cum simplici atque amabili decore Saulii: antecedit verem, (ver) neque opus habet vermibus serici textoribus: ipsa ramos suos atque folia vestit lanugine Sericea tenuissima, quam nulli noverunt vermes.*

* It should be SALICIS   This Description is extracted from *Theophili Sigefridi Bayeri* MUSAEUM SINICUM. Tom, I. p. 130. Petropoli. 1730.

Ad

The Willow and the Peach Tree.

From a *Chinese* TALE.

THE Spring appear'd, and hush'd was ev'ry Wind,

When the smooth *Willow*, o'er the Stream reclin'd,

Cheer'd by the Ray that animates the Globe,

Throws, o'er her yellow Bark, a verdant Robe.

Dash'd at the Beauties which her Foliage spread,

The Rival *Peach-Tree*, blushing, bends his Head:

Enrag'd, his Flowers with varying Lustre grac'd,

He tears; and scatters round the lovely Waste.

The *Willow*, proud of milder Charms, outvies

The Flashing Splendor of the brightest Dyes.

Gay Harbinger of Spring, she scorns the aid

Of toiling Silk Worms, and is self-array'd;

Decking her Sprays, and Zephyr-dancing Leaves

With Down more soft than the fam'd Insect weaves.

Ad

Ad * Amicos.

TErram perpetuo rotare motu

Si quis perneget, ô boni sodales,

Sumat millia multa poculorum:

Postque millia multa poculorum,

Terram perpetuo rotare motu,

Seque cum volucri rotare terrâ

Certus asseret, ô boni sodales

* Poetæ Rusticantis literatum Otium, p 28. Londini 1713

Sur

The Earth's Motion prov'd.

S O N G.

Set to Mufick by Mr. *Leveridge.*

MY joyous Blades, with Rofes crown'd,

    Who quaff bright Nectar at its Spring,

Difpute not, if the Earth goes round,

    But hear a thirfty Poet fing.

All take your Glaffes, charge them high ;

    Let Bumpers fwiftly Bumpers chace :

Each Man drink fifty, foon you'll fpy

    The Earth wheel round with rapid Pace.

On

Sur Mad^{lle.} *Camargo* & fur Mad^{lle} *Sallé*,
danfant enfemble a l'Opera de *Paris*.

Impromptu, par M. de Voltaire.

AH! *Camargo que vous êtes brillante !*

Mais que Sallé, grands Dieux, eft raviffante !

Que vos Pas font legers, mais que les fiens font doux !

Elle eft inimitable, & vous etes nouvelle :

Les Nymphes fautent comme Vous,

Mais les Graces danfent comme Elle.

On Mad^lle *Camargo*, and Mad^lle *Sallé*, dancing together in the Opera House at *Paris*.

An extempore Epigram, from the French *of* Mr. de Voltaire.

YOUR Charms, *Camargo*, dart Delight,
But *Sallé* ravishes the Sight.

Your flying Step the Dance improves,

With shining Ease she sweetly moves.

Gay Novelty attracts in You,

Her, we inimitable View.

You, like the sprightly Wood-Nymphs bound,

She, like the Graces, skims the Ground.

Soeur Jeanne. CONTE.

Tiré de la Fontaine.

SOEUR Jeanne ayant fait un Poupon,

Jeûnoit, vivoit en sainte fille ;

Toûjours êtoit en oraison,

Et toûjours ses soeurs à la Grille.

Un jour donc l'Abesse leur dit,

Vivez comme soeur Jeanne vit ;

Fuyez le monde & sa sequelle.

Toutes reprirent à l'instant ;

Nous serons aussi sages qu'elle,

Quand nous en aurons fait autant.

Dame

Dame J A N E, or the penitent Nun, (written in 1720) set to Musick by the late Mr. *Haym*.

A Nun there was, as Primrose gay,
And form'd of very yielding Clay,

Who long had resolutely strove

To guard against the Shafts of Love,

Till Cupid whisp'ring soft the Fair,

Her pious *Vow* dissolves in Air.——

The stolen Sweets she now would smother;

In vain——poor *Jenny*'s made a Mother.

These youthful Pranks quite giv'n o'er,

Sighing, she cries, " I'll sin no more;

" No more become Man's sensual Prey,

" But spend in Prayer each fleeting Day."——

Lo!

Lo¹ in her Cell ſhe weeping lies,

Nor from the Croſs once moves her Eyes;

Whilſt Siſters, tittering at the Grate,

Paſs all their Hours in wanton Prate,

The Abbeſs overjoy'd to find

This bliſsful Change in *Jenny*'s Mind,

With Face demure, the Girls addreſſing,

" Ah Daughters! if you hope—a Bleſſing,

" From righteous *Jane* Example take;

" The World, its Pomps, and Joys forſake."——

" Ay— ſo we will,"— cries ev'ry Nun——

" When we,—— as righteous *Jane* have done."

ODE.

O D E.

Par Mr. *de Voltaire.* 1715.

AUX *maux les plus affreux le Ciel nous abandonne,*
La Discorde, la faim, la Mort nous environne,

Et les Dieux contre nous soulevés tant de fois,

Equitables vangeurs des Crimes de la Terre

Ont *frappé du Tonnerre*

Les Peuples & les Roys.

Des plaines de Tortose au bord du Boristhene

Mars a conduit son char attelé par la haine;

Les vents contagieux ont volé sur ses pas,

Et soufflant de la Mort les Semences funestes,

Ont devoré les restes

Echapés aux Combats.

D'un

D'un Monarque puiſſant la Race fortunée

Rempliſſoit de leur Nom l'Europe conſternée.

J'ay paſſé. De la Terre ils etoient diſparus,

Et le Peuple abatu que ſa miſere etonne

    Les cherche au pied du Trone

    Et ne les trouve plus.

Peuples reconnoiſſés la main qui vous accable,

Ce n'eſt point des Deſtins l'arrêt irrevocable,

Ceſt le courroux des Dieux mais facile a calmer ;

Merites d'etre heureux, oſés quitter le vice,

    C'eſt par ce ſacrifice

    Qu'on les peut deſarmer.

Rome

Rome en sages Heros autrefois si fertile,

Qui fut des plus grands Roys la terreur & l'Asile,

Rome fut vertueuse & dompta l'Univers ;

Mais l'Orgueil & le luxe enfans de la Victoire,

    Du comble de la Gloire

    La plongerent aux Fers.

Quoy? verra t'on toûjours de ces Tirans Serviles,

Oppresseurs insolents des Veuves, des Pupiles,

Elever des Palais dans nos Champs desolés?

Verrai-je cimenter leurs portiques durables

    Du sang des miserables

    Devant eux immolés?

Elevés

Elevés dans le sein de l'infame Avarice,

Leurs Enfans ont succé le lait de l'Injustice,

Et dans nos Tribunaux vont juger les Humains.

Malheur à qui fondé sur sa foible Innocence,

A mis son esperance

Dans leurs indignes mains.

Des Nobles cependant l'Ambition captive

S'endort entre les bras de la Molesse oisive,

Et ne porte aux combats que des Corps languissans.

Cesses, abandonnés à des mains plus vaillantes

Ces piques trop pesantes

Pour vos Bras impuissans.

Voyés

Voyés cette Beauté fous les yeux de fa mere,

Elle apprend en naiffant l'art dangereux de plaire,

Et d'irriter en nous de funeftes penchants.

Son enfance previent le tems d'etre coupable,

  Le vice trop aimable

  Inftruit fes premiers Ans.

Bientot bravant les yeux de l'Epoux qu'elle outrage,

Elle abandonne aux mains d'un Courtifan volage,

De fes trompeurs appas le Charme empoifonneur.

Que dis-je! cet Epoux à qui l'himen la lie,

  Trafiquant l'Infamie

  La livre au Defhonneur.

Ainfi

Ainſi vous outragés les Dieux & la Nature,

O que ce n'etoit pas de cette ſource impure

Qu'on vit naitre ces Francs des Scithes ſucceſſeurs,

Qui du char d'Attila detachant la Fortune

  De la Cauſe commune

  Furent les Deffenſeurs.

Le Citoyen alors ſçavoit porter les Armes :

Sa fidele Moitié qui negligeoit ſes Charmes

Pour ſon retour heureux preparoit des Lauriers ;

Recevoit dans ſes mains ſa Cuiraſſe ſanglante,

  Et ſa hache fumante

  Du trépas des Guerriers.

Au travail endurcis, leur superbe courage

Ne prodigua jamais une imbecile homage

A de vaines Beautés qui ne les touchoient pas ;

Et d'un sexe timide & né pour la Molesse

Ils plaignoient la foiblesse

Et ne l'adoroient pas.

Dans ces sauvages tems l'heroique Rudesse,

Leur laissoit ignorer la delicate adresse

D'excuser les forfaits par un subtil detour.

Jamais on n'entendit leur bouche peu sincere

Donner a l'Adultere

Le tendre nom d'Amour.

Mais

Mais insensiblement l'adroite Politesse

Des Cœurs effeminés souveraine maitresse,

Effaça de nos Mœurs l'austere Pureté,

Et du subtil Mensonge empruntant l'artifice,

  Bientot à l'Injustice

  Donna l'air d'equité.

Le Luxe a ses cotés marche avec arrogance,

L'Or qui nait sous ses pas s'écoule en sa presence,

Le fol Orgueil le suit compagnon de l'erreur,

Il sappe des Etats la Grandeur souveraine

  De leur Chûte prochaine

  Brillant avant-coureur.

4 AU 64

F I N I S.

CPSIA information can be obtained
at www.ICGtesting.com
Printed in the USA
LVOW04s1349291117
558021LV00011B/186/P